# Chimes

Also by Michael Dennis Browne

*The Wife of Winter*
*Sun Exercises*
*The Sun Fetcher*
*Smoke from the Fires*
*Selected Poems 1965-1995*
*You Won't Remember This*
*Give Her the River*
*Things I Can't Tell You*
*Panthers*
*What the Poem Wants*
*The Voices*

# Chimes

Selected Shorter Poems

*Michael Dennis Browne*

**NODIN PRESS**

ISBN: 978-1-947237-00-1
Cover art: Joyce Lyon
Design: John Toren

Library of Congress Cataloging-in-Publication Data–
Names: Browne, Michael Dennis, author.
Title: Chimes / Michael Dennis Browne.
Description: Minneapolis, MN : Nodin Press, 2017.
Identifiers: LCCN 2017045032 | ISBN 9781947237001
Classification: LCC PR6052.R618 A6 2017 | DDC 821/.914--dc23
LC record available at https://lccn.loc.gov/2017045032

Published by
Nodin Press
5114 Cedar Lake Road,
Minneapolis, MN 55416
*www.nodinpress.com*

*"Souls of poets dead and gone"*

## Acknowledgements

I would like to thank the editors of magazines and anthologies who have published some of these poems over the past fifty years or so;

Carnegie Mellon University Press (Gerald Costanzo, Cynthia Lamb) for exceptional support over many years;

Norton Stillman for his initiative with this collection and for his longtime support of Minnesota writers;

John Toren for his always thoughtful attention;

Wilber Schilling of Indulgence Press for the beautifully designed *Panthers*;

and Joyce Lyon, old friend, for her exquisite cover art.

I am grateful to you all.

# Contents

## 1

## 2

*3*

5

*6*

*1*

# Driving South, Sunset, February

House on fire, but only the glass
Fence on fire, but only the wires

Horse on fire, but only the eyes

# Meteors, August

Some spurt, some sputter,
some make a long easy arc
before they are done.
This loose fire among the fixed
we lie on our backs and wait for:
this able-to-fall,
this able-to-flame-and-be-gone.

# Watching Rushing Water

the water knows who you are

the gulls are going
for everything thrown

but all the acids
of that dark water

the rankness, the pouring

the imperceptible
wearing away of stone

they know who you are

# Cottonwoods

they call them
   the trees of life
      and you can see why

when you lie on your back
   and narrow your eyes
      and peer

you will see they are
   rivers in air
      with everything flowing

and all of their branches
   emptying
      into heaven

# Maternal

Let the fly-catcher build
where she wants, where she will;
that bird is no serpent,
and our eaves hers.

While that other is locked
to an upper branch,
looking out, looking down,
listening as night comes on
for her fallen,

the light beginning to fail
and somewhere below in the woodland
her young hawk walking.

# North

3 AM, I'm instant awake—Lord,
I've left the car in the ramp in town
with the children inside, with the engine
on as I ran . . . No, that's not . . . left it
at a meter on Washington,
just under a NO PARKING sign,
the cops by now . . .

No . . . slow down . . . look, the children
are here, count them, they're fine,
look, the car's here, we made it,
we're four hours north of town,
and listen—a bird just began . . .
now it's stopped. Damn. I'll
have to jump up, go jam
more coins in that pine.

# Harvest Moon

I thought you would be more
the color of crops;
I thought you might earn your name.
But if you entered a bar,
each livid face would turn
and stare at you.

Why do sink your vast ghost
body so close to us? You seem about
to pry mere pines apart.
How near dare you?

You look like nothing to nourish us,
no muse nor mother
with your scabby seas.
But if you have something in you
for our curing, come down.

## One of My Trees

One of my trees has caught the moon.
An aspen, not a memorable one—
you know, a popple.

                          I don't care

if it's there in the morning or not—
one of my trees has caught the moon,
there's yellow all over its upper body.

                          I don't mind

if it doesn't last long—
one of my trees has caught the moon.

# Wash Wish

what the tree means when
there's a grief in the air

*wash*　　　　*wish*

by the tree I mean the pine
by the pine I mean the moan

*wash*　　　　*wish*

by the leaves I mean the needles
by the needles I mean the pain

*wash*　　　　*wish*

whenever some swaying
of making of mourn to be done

# The House Without Us

Creatures must surely come closer than now
as we sit in a circle of lawn chairs,
quiet under August stars,
some fixed, some falling.

Sometimes I'd like to be something
a little less than human,
to be able to watch
as the bear sways up
to rub her rump upon the siding,
to rub her shadow up against our absence.

Leaves, one day I'll be one of you
rather than even the most neighborly star,
nearer to those we'll have left
and all *they* love,
they, too, encircled under these same heavens
but in some later August of the world.

## To the Leaf, October

You are like something the sun
has fashioned from its own
flesh, and lets hang here. You
are scarcely solid. I could dream
you dissolve on my tongue.
I do not try
to touch you or take you.

# The Bat That Got into the House

you will want to know what I did
after I found it stuck to the fly-paper
and fallen with it into the bath-tub,
after I watched it struggle and squeal,
the sickly glue-stuff half chewed through
and one wing waving. reader, I drowned it.

# Gulls, Fools

gulls echo
what the fools say

when the fools spray
dead bread

the gulls
go for it

# North Shore

gulls' cries lace
my shoes of stone

*2*

# A Visit

My parents visited me
in the form of a river;
I felt the force of that river's flood
up my spine, as though
my back were the socket to receive
my parents' double power.

I grinned like a madman in a gale.

Then my mother and father
began together to braid
the hair of my life behind me.

# At the Convent

I dance with my pearly dad
I twirl with my auntie the nun

I eat the awful sandwiches

# Dad

his keyboards, his quick fingers
his feet in dancing pumps on the pedals

the schooner Toccata
the sloop Fugue

deer running through the church

# Forest of Dean

our mother walks
    into the trees
until we see her
    no more

we follow, walk
    where she walked
bend to touch
    the flowers

she grows
    as she goes

# Mum

I talk to her often;
scared on the street,

I say: *Come on now, Mum,*
*help your son.*

I wait for the cars to relax,
and then I cross.

## To My Brother Peter on the Birth of his First Child

You who love to climb
the mountains you live among,
now you are roped to someone;
and when one day you fall,
as you will,
why, you've a son to swing from.

## Mary My Sister

help Mary in drowned heaven
our safe little remember stream children
cloud watercress shadow buttercup long grass
farm sky tremble willow oak leaning
your crown of wet thorns

# Night Thought

Awake, I think of being
　　out on the moors
in the gale, the rain.
　　I scare myself back
to sleep with that thought.

Where do the sheep go
　　that are loose? Where
do the horses go? What
　　do the rocks do?
(Huddle, huddle, huddle.)

I know what the streams do:
　　they go on boiling
coldly, like the rage among
　　members of a family.

# English

When I hear the wind, I think of England,
    I think of the wind as an English thing,
the way when I was a boy
    I thought of life as an English thing.
But even now, so along the years,
    when the wind starts moaning around the house,
when the windows rattle, so that Nellie
    startled, says, "Dad, what's that?",
I know what it is; I know it's something
    that still can strum the soundest home,
an early thing, still alive and well,
    and, truth to tell, as wild as ever
from out of a life so long ago English.

# The Anxiety

I don't expect the anxiety to go away
    but I want the anxiety to know
its place in the scheme of things
    of which I seem to consist.
I want the anxiety to be
    not an attention-getter or star
but faceless, like a butler bringing trays,
    whose old hand has turned down my bed,
the one I could even come to pity,
    this trembling retainer I keep on,
as my father before me,
    out of some kind of long-standing
loyalty to the anxiety family,
    whose fortunes have been bound up
with ours for so long.

# Kin

you are all my kin

in the small hours
I claim you

set out in your shadow boats
by sail, by paddle, by oar

we'll meet
on a vastness of water

however wild it may be

all of you my kin
and I claim you

# Wood Dove, Surrey

*(with granddaughter Julia)*

away in the leaves
she calls

*yes, you were once*
*little here*

she calls    she calls

*you must know*
*the sorrow goes on*

she calls    she calls    she calls

*and now you know*
*about the joy*

# Rose Cottage, Blackheath

Hovering close, hoping
some red-faced owner
will storm out yelling
"you're trespassing!"

so I can say back,
"we lived here . . .
seventy-five years ago . . .
I was two . . ."
but no one to notice,
no one
to swat me away.

Now out again
along the paths,
among the ten thousand things,
all my old secrets
seething in me.

# My Brother with Flowers

my brother for our pain arriving with flowers
my brother with his own pain arriving

we, of four, the two living left
our parents' flowers, us

my brother the other flower arriving
and the flowers of his tears

his tears, our tears, a meeting of waters
today my brother with flowers arriving

## What Was Said When the Brothers and Sisters Were in the Same Room Together for the First Time in Ten Years

if this was a hundred years ago
we would all have lived in the same village
we would have been able to help one another
we would have seen one another all the time

*3*

# River

one day the midwife
    bent over and was busy

and then my river
    of a boy began

# His Toys

We planned to keep your first toys,
preserve them; one day,
when you were grown, lead you
to a secret closet, watch you
pull wide, amazed,
re-discover your treasures.
But we can't: you're eating them.

# Dancing for Him

He likes to watch us dance, we do it
for him, he laughs, we waltz
around him in the kitchen or polka,
leaping, through the living room, he
laughs, or cheek to cheek like
a dragged-out marathon couple we
slouch and stagger, he throws back
his months' old head and laughs.

What he'll remember of these times,
who knows? Maybe one morning,
waking from a dream of faces,
he'll turn to one beside him, saying:
"That's it! They used to dance for me!"

# Peter and Thunder

Your face when you heard it. How you looked up.
How, crouched over toy parts,
suddenly you stiffened. How then you turned,
how you stared up in the direction
of the thunder. *They are at the gates.*
How then you looked at me, as if
I might send them away, as if with a few
low-toned, well-chosen words I could
send the thunder gangs scuttling back
through all the holes in the sky.
As if there were no thunder deep
down in my own bones, no thunder
in yours, little son.

# My Rage

My rage can scare my little son.
My dad's could me. He startles, stares.
Quickly I calm. That's it, it's done.
Father, forgive.
My rage can scare my little son.

# Gulf War Dream

our legless son arriving home from school
demanding to know what's on TV, which cartoons,
rings under his eyes, his seven-year-old
face pitiless: *what's on? what's on?*

*first,* I say, *before TV, tell me*
*how you are, give me a hug, did this*
*happen to you in school today? tell me,*
*who did this to you? look at me.*

he doesn't want to talk about it,
doesn't want to look, to touch, it seems
the wounds are old, it seems he gets by
quite nicely on his hands,

and pushing past me toward the TV,
white-faced, raging: *what's on? what's on?*

# Holy Week

With our son at the Basilica,
the laying on of hands,
a long line,
the priest intense each time
with each of us,
vestmented arms outstretched,
eyes closed, head bowed,
murmuring.

Always a little behind
with everything.
Waking at 4 am.

# In Chicago

Calling early, I wake you
from deep inside a dream;
*it's weird, Dad,* you say,

*you just came into my room*
*with an alarm clock and a doll,*
*and you were wearing dark glasses.*

I used to think I could never be
as memorable to you
as my own vivid dad to me,

but now there I am in Chicago,
in your dreams, and such
good things I am bringing you.

# In Summer

Hard on these summer mornings to tell,
While windows flicker and rafters weave,
While handles hover and shingles swim,
What's real, what's seem, what's maybe-believe.

Shadows and leaves and light are the vessels,
That fever their murmurs along the floor,
That riddle these rivers across our drowsing,
That make us a daughter at our door.

# Good Friday, 6 a.m., Devon, Listening to Mary and the Blackbird

Even a father would not say
You cause the sun to clamber up,
All sinew, from the valley floor;
No, not for any songs of yours
But chimed by them, he'll slowly rise
To roll the granite mist aside.
O even a father could not say
You cause the sun to climb.

# With Nellie

If she were a flower, she'd be red.
If a tree, oak.
And a cookie?
"I'd be a Valentine's Cookie."
And what sort of water
would you want to be?
"I'm a river," says Nellie.

# March Morning

Two little girls
coming down the sidewalk
dragging egg-cartons on strings,
two clothes-pins stuck
to the front of each carton,
one at the back,
and when I ask them
what they are up to,
they yell:
> "The bugs are coming!"
> The bugs are coming!"

# Fire

You love a fire; you love to sit and watch
    the little fires float up toward the larger,
you love how dark is torn awhile
    by something ragged you've begun
with paper twists, with scraps, with twigs,
    how leaves are shaking all about you,
and down the hill the owl is calling, calling.
    You chatter, joke, wave sticks. Your eyes shine,
and it is summer still, on earth our home,
    as always in that other land we dream of
with *its* fires, *its* children. You are twelve
    as I write this; you are ten (just); you are seven.

# Child's Elm Song

If there were no trees
I would take my turn
And stand in the street in spring
With arms wide open
In case there were birds
Who needed a place to sing.

# Light upon the Water

Like the light upon the water,
    Summer in the swaying tree,
Radiance of the woken flower,
    You are these and more to me.

From this hour, from this moment
    Where we make our holy vow,
No more distant, no more hidden,
    We are undivided now.

Life before us, love within us
    More than we can sing or say,
Everything is grace, is given,
    All our dreams begin this day.

# Call

once a day call yourself up

that huge laugh others hear
coming at you from yourself

you hearing
you laughing

# Music and the Rain

When I'm alone
   I like to listen
      to music and the rain.

When I'm with you
   I like to listen
      to music and the rain.

What would Mozart say,
   d'you suppose,
      if he heard us listening

to (his) music and the rain?
   Just what would that
      indefatigable child say?

(You think the rain
   was born brilliant, I think
      it became that way.)

*4*

# Invitation

I've been invited
to the White House

to a ceremony
in the rose garden

to receive a medal
for anxiety

I'm not going

# Lizard

someone in me like a lizard
someone who licks his lips

someone cold
like the king of lizards in his sheath

# In Me

I sense that someone in me
has always been pleased

with my life, feel I should
reprove the pleased one

for his senseless
permissiveness, learn

his secrets.

# Queens

several of the queens of England
hide in me

in fear
for their barren lives

several of Henry's queens
trembling

# Evening

mornings strung out in me

bouncing across the bay
like brisk little whitecaps

their sails filled
with invisible Spirit

but it's evening

# Hurrying

someone hurrying to bring
   whatever it was
we once wanted, now
   have no hunger for

the call must be going out
   from somewhere in us
*more, more, more*
   but our needs are few.

# Falling Asleep in the Afternoon

Again I am
falling asleep in the afternoon,
not "falling in love again," but
falling asleep in the afternoon.
The glass in the window thickens
until only the room is mine,
and then the room inside the room,
through which I begin to run.

# The Things You Think You Hear

one night a wedding
with bells
but the street is empty

one January
the watering
of a garden, even

the silky dripping
from leaf to lower
leaf

in the library, late,
the opening of a gift
a child's hands

rushing
through soft paper

# After Anna Swir

old pearl with no shine
old shine of the subtle secret

old brain of pearl
old pearly Bible of one page

pearl infant asleep
pearl dog dreaming

pearly scripture gleaming
impenetrable pearl masterpiece

# Horses

keep hearing them
along the river

making the leaves crack
making the coins spin

in the streets
of the city of horses

where it is always
raining or grieving

# Beater

your dad drives some old car
I seen him

your dad's old, too
I seen the rust on him

got a convertible head
know what I mean?

yeah I seen
the rust on him

# Key

when a key
dies

its door
doesn't

go to
the funeral

# Knock, Knock

the i can't help it
is at the door
shall we admit it?
yes yes of course shrieks
the what else is new

## Still Wondering

which parts
of the dark

are not meant
to be mended

# Melody

Blind Melody brought to your door.
She must be with you for a while;
tell no one of this guest you hold.

You will know when she must leave
when you yourself can see no longer,
and only with her gone can you begin

the singing which was once against
your will, your power, your dream,
but is now your meaning.

# Dogs

I remember I have forgotten
our old dogs

like a prayer I have been
too lazy to say

now once again
here they are

running along
in the dark

# Ivory-Billed Woodpecker

return of the legendary
*Lord God Bird*

you who will
one day

wipe away
all tears

# My Rain

I heard you last night

My wife went out in you to give our son's friend
    a ride home
I wondered, if she were never to return, could I
    ever forgive you?

I love seeing the young, the waves and waves
    of them

I don't envy the young
I love them as I love the rain

The rain that also bewilders me
The exhausting rain

Sometimes I feel like dry old grass

Then comes my rain

*5*

# Owl

*to John Berryman*

*On November 30<sup>th</sup>, 1972, a Great Horned Owl was seen high*
*in a tree on the University of Minnesota campus between Wal-*
*ter Library and Johnston Hall. The owl stayed here all day; by*
*the following morning, he was gone.*

He is there, with his large eyes,
high above us,
who were never close.
He will not say, he will not say
what it is he wants.
But we are glad he is there,
we without wings.
There is nothing he need not do.
And if he jumps,
we need not fear for him.

# Neighbor in May

my neighbor is hammering
and mending his house
he fixes in almost a frenzy
by night he dreams of his wife
dead nearly a year now
he dreams of nailing and healing
he dreams of repairing the damage

# October Prayer

When it seems there is so
  much to be done

and how little there is I can do,

I calm to become
  the cottonwood's wrinkled bark

and not the millions of crows

I once would have been,
  straining their raw voices

so high in the tree of life.

Help me, help me again,
  my only God.


*for Dietrich Reinhart OSB*

## Dietrich in the Pure Land

How cold that pine box must quickly have become.
We had stepped forward to spill dark earth onto the lid.
I slept poorly that night within sight of the cemetery.
The animated man is gone,
there is no seeing him, there is only
the doing to be done of the ways he followed.
That box holds no living water.
The River Dietrich flows on in an elsewhere of fire.

# Like Him, Like My Dead Shepherd

This summer I grow
heavy like him,

my bones thicken,
my mass increases.

Wading out of the lake,
I shake myself,

shake shake shake
till the white hairs fly.

Home again, I settle
down on the floor

in the corner
with a groan.

## Last Ice, Mid-April

Not even the children, bringing
their children, visit. Even
the nurses are turned away.
He lies there, gleaming.

# Dream at the Death of James Wright

The wind is rolling the buffalo down,
the wind is shining and sharpening the buffalo
and rolling them down.
The sheep have already scattered
toward the forest, sheep are streaming
along the stained edges of the forest,
but the wind is rolling the buffalo down.
We have built no shelter for them,
we have put up no corral.
They don't know enough to
come together, bind their black fur
together, sit out the storm.
I see one huge one struggling
inside a lantern of grasses.
The wind is rolling the buffalo down,
shining and sharpening them
and rolling them down.

# The Old Man and the Poem

you are the old man and the poem
you are the old poem who went on
beyond the words beyond the breath
(little wishbone of a breastbone
ceasing its negligible motion)

I am who kept on saying
the words to you who went on
into the no breath beyond
the poem's breathing and your friend

who wear now what you wore
now wrap your robe around me
as wind rattles the window
easily rattled the window and the reader

but never your beyond of breath
nor ever the saying the singing
that so long ago once
we were dreamed into being

*Chester Anderson 1923–2006*

# The Old Happiness

bring back the old happiness
you remember the one

no inner organs laboring
no struggling of the years to come

at yesterday's service for a man
who ended his life, then lingered

the best moment not the kindly
sprightly silver pastor

but the trio of grandchildren
swaying doing a Beatles number

pretty much on key and warbling away
in the dialect of the old happiness

# For Kilian at Ninety

In a glade in the summer woods
　　I see you standing.

Everything fluttering, humming, fragrant.

How did you come to be here?
　　You walked, of course,

as you walk everywhere.

I can imagine nothing that you need to do
　　after the miles, the years,

save to belong on this holy ground,

all distances, all that was ever beyond,
　　now gathered within,

your flesh a Lamp through which
　　the spacious spirit, pure being,

shines.

*for Kilian McDonnell OSB*

# In a Dark Time

the best thing
in the Roethke movie

not the poetry

Ted in the kitchen
at the sink

sweats, paunchy

sipping coffee
looking out the window

at the leaves

the wrinkled eyes
over the wet rim

of the lifted cup

watching

# Mourning

only need to hear the voice
the hidden one who calls and calls
no need to see the very dove
to be reminded why I grieve

# Hallowe'en 1971

I carve my first head. Then I carve another.
Now I have two Vietnamese
children on my table.

I place a candle in each of them, & light it.
The heads are still wet inside. I've put
the seeds in a brown bag.

I take one head to the window.
The other I put on the stair, with the front
door open. By it, a bowl of candy.

2

Down the block,
round the neighborhood,
all over this darkened country,
the hollow yellow heads
burning in windows, & tiny
American ghosts running toward them
through the dark with open hands.

# Dandelion, Meltdown

At first, the spectacular gold.
How fast it rusts to white
then is gone, ghost by ghost,
in a mere wind.

Let us go and sit with our old
bald mother the earth a while,
let her mumble and ramble, as she will,
of her skies and seas.

Bring the young.

*(time of Chernobyl)*

# The Face

I wonder what war would do to the face of the world,
    more war, I mean, more and more.
I wonder whose face the world is (I believe I know
    whose body it is), but I touch
the face of the world in the dark as if I were
    blindfolded, playing "Meet the Giant" again
with my Uncle Bim, knew he was soon to take
    my finger, say *here's the giant's eye*, plunge it
into the half of an orange he was holding.

I feel around in the dark on the face of the world;
    I wonder what war would do
to the mouth, whether more teeth will go,
    whether the mouth will be raw
with new wounds, or dry as never before
    with sores of the old fears.

# I Believe Anita Hill

Darkness is falling

That microphone clipped
To his lapel

Could be a twig or a stick beetle
Or even a snail

Were this not a senate hearing
But the forest floor

Something is crawling

# Thieves

Men will dress as bears as snakes
    to grapple to cripple to crush to pry
men will not dress as sparrows as thrushes
    as finches to fly
men will dress as eagles as owls as falcons as hawks
    to strip to strain to stain to strike

# Woe

*Woe*, you say.
   *Woe out, about. Woe roams.*

You reach into your pockets
   to jingle the small coins there
but they are woe.

There is woe on your cheeks,
   there is woe in your hair.
A lone bird rowing her wings
   calls *woe woe woe*
all across the air.

Your woe was once
   in a locked box, but now
it is everywhere.

# Your Sister

*Do not cast me off in old age; forsake me not*
*when my strength is spent.*

– Psalm 71: 9

Walt, Walt, when you've a moment,
   come by the room of Ruth the poet,
gone from her spacious house, her garden
   with its ranks of roses,
(this day her birthday, also yours,
   she a mere eighty-one, and you
one hundred and eighty-three),
   and as once you did with those young wounded
who called to you as you entered—
   fresh-clothed, combed, your beard perfumed—
step into the silence of cut blooms
   where one sits with padded hands
and wheelchair and her shards of speech,
   come, *companero,* if you can,
from shadow, murmur some words,
   lay your lilac hand on her head
that's still like a lion's, kiss your sister.

*for Ruth Roston*

# Shall We Gather

Where twisted lengths of girders
   Lie along the riverbank
They seem like scraps of sky
   That dropped, dragging
Its birds with them

And these were people
   Unknown, loved,
Who flew awhile
   (As everyone dreams to do)
In this world of falling

*Highway 35 Bridge*
*August 1, 2007, Minneapolis*

# Voice Lesson

*in memory of Krista Sandstrom, singer*

all the years are a voice lesson
there is so much to sing
we need every instrument

so we may sound the depths
of where we are, how we are
ever to know one another

no lanterns of moons I know
to send across the evening sky
other than music

no petals to set in procession
upon the breathing stream
save our songs

all the years a voice lesson
there is so much to sing
we need every instrument

# Nocturnal

"I was never beaten by any parent,
but the nights beat me."

– Sofia Kenosis

*the sun goes*

down
on our street

and in the dark
the red

buildings
shimmer

*jazz bandage*

dusk
as the words begin
their slide

and the evening
    of meaning
        is here

*small hours*

Is that dust on your sleep or gold?
Is that sleep on your eyes or dust?
Is that flesh on your arm or bone?

*panthers*

seen
   running
      among
         the
            meanings

*beach*

I was on a beach
I was a wild stone

the wind blew me
all about the world

though I was stone

*northern Ireland dream*

The child began to slap me.
Her hands grew larger, harder,
became a man's, a sapper's,
rigging quick traps. She whirled
about me, spun, tossed
flowers on my eye-graves, tombed
me with slaps. When I tried
to speak to her, she exploded.

*dirt*

I like to talk dirt to the road
I have a mucky mouth filled with gaps
I have mud for a dog
and a broken leash understanding

*liminal*

His Holiness
desires to know
how you want your
enchilada

the grave asks,
*will this do?*

*the man*

A man comes in the door
who makes your skin shiver.
He says: *I want the television.*
You say: *Have it.*
He says: *I want the dog.*
*The dog*, you say, *is more difficult.*

You wrestle, he is fast
he is all over you,
his nails rip your back.
*Darling*, you say.

He tears the stocking from his head
and is the girl of your dreams.

*not that*

I dreamed I was a bird.
Not that there was flight.
Instead I stood
on my two claws and pecked
at some dark meat on the ground.
You'd have to turn off the highway
and down dirt roads to find me.
Not that I recommend it.
Not that I was of the kind who sings.
Not that the bird had wings.

*brother dream*

walking with you slowly
over the trembling green

our feet seeming to float
as once they used to

my satchel dense
with old coins

your face in profile
on one side

mine
on the other

### Olivier

Olivier came to see me, eager for
tips for the interpretation of his new role.
We sat in my walled garden.
"By evening," Olivier said, "I will be
in Stuttgart. By the way, can you get
a hot dog around here
en route to the airport?"
"Know about Coney Dogs?" I asked.
Olivier's eyes lit up.
"You can get them around here somewhere,"
I said—"at 91st and Swabsworth, I believe."
"That's exact enough for a dream," Olivier said.

And then: "You're terrific. Now I'll know
how to play the part."
Soon, he was in Stuttgart.

*your hair*

I love your hair.
I love how your hair
shines. I love how your hair
rows
across the Atlantic

# Daddy

*autumn*

I like these soft wet days.
    I'm reminded of England.

I haven't had an autumn day
    in more than thirty years.

It seems we're near the sea,
    ours a port city,
these sparrows gulls.

I like this silk of yellow weather.
    I feel my father near.

*street*

I think I see my father in the street.
It's just the back of his head, but I know it's him.
I race down the driveway, yelling "Daddy! Daddy!"
the way my colt of a son cries out to me

when he's in need. One turn, one smile would heal
all years of his being gone. But no, it's just
some frail unknown, carefully navigating
the glacial waters of the neighborhood.

*1954*

Sunday. Fall asleep on a Sunday.
Lie down by a fire and doze.
After mass, in a slack little chair,
or there on the floor; we'll comb
your hair till it gleams, we'll
give you wings. Sunday.
Fall asleep on a Sunday.
By a fire, in a slack little chair,
or there on the floor.

*fear of*

not knowing where things are
I don't know where I put
my pen, my glasses.

I don't know where my father is

*pipe*

my father hands
the pipe to me

*peace* says my father
and leans down the years

(I am his any
blue smoke son)

*and pass it on*

*slender*

the slender sky my father
the hills the stream the wood doves' calling
the echo in the valley
of the lily's cry my father

*leaves*

From my father's glass I sip
through my father's glass I spy
all my father's crows are calling
all my father's leaves are flying

*among trees, moonlight*

my dad could be here
Eddie of the wood
Father of Leaves

# Cabin

fell asleep
  as I'd wanted to
    on the wind

became the branches
  leaping about
    I'd dreamed to be

flew by myself
  too fast
    for myself to see

*late March*

I hear old winter hanged himself;
I heard it from three crows going over.
Not that they were telling it to me
personally; any fool could receive
such news in that echoing landscape.

*cabin, cry*

startled at the squeal
    of brakes in the driveway—
somebody's here!—
    but no, just some
harsh bird back there
    in the yellowing woods,
its mechanical cry

    *rain*

it sounds as if someone is coming
    *it is the rain*
it sounds as if we have guests
    *it is the rain*
set out, anyway, some extra plates
    *it is the rain*

*dark*

too dark
to walk

but the dog
wants to

*country secrets*

What do the dirt roads do
when nobody's looking?
Roll over
and kiss the ditches!

*like two snakes*

like two snakes in the grass
shiny you, shiny me
then we sleep

*in the May woods*

I'm out in the woods
   got nothing to say
just want to watch
   I'll be here all day

*bird, 3:47 AM*

just got the part
wants everyone
to know it

*once again*

my dog and the moon
know it is Spring
once again they can see
their white faces in the water

*summer*

Fell asleep under a tree.
Or the tree fell
asleep over me. Dark old pine.
Both of us dreaming.

*in August*

                as if one afternoon
        the summer begins
    to accept her age
the lines in
her face ease
    and yellowjackets
        begin to wander
                out of the crevices

*September*

now smoke begins to flower
    above the cosmos
that are past their prime

dry sticks fit only
  for the fires

and little melons
  that will never
reach a mouth

  *when the deer reminds me of my son*

when I go out and he is there
  (storm door bangs behind)

when he startles in the clearing
  begins to run

when he bounds off through the brush

when he is gone

  *old pines*

old pines pretending
we were never here

*balcony, evening*

watching the leaves shiver
letting the little leaves go

sounds of our neighbor Lou
still mowing below

no way to say
to the shadows: *no*

   *not to be here*
(title from a line by Philip Larkin)

not to be here. to be otherwhere.
   (the leaves tremble, it is
      the middle of the night.)
not to have leaves. not to need
   leaves for my joy.

Michael Dennis Browne was born in England, of mostly Irish ancestry, in 1940, and has lived in the United States since 1965. Two of his collections have won the Minnesota Book Award for poetry. As a librettist and lyricist he has written many texts for music, working for almost four decades with composer Stephen Paulus; their best-known shorter works include "Pilgrims' Hymn," "The Road Home," "Hymn to the Eternal Flame" and "Hymn for America." *To Be Certain of the Dawn*, a post-Holocaust oratorio (BIS Records), was nominated for the Pulitzer Prize in music by the Minnesota Orchestra. He has recently worked with Craig Hella Johnson on the fusion oratorio *Considering Matthew Shepard*. Browne taught at Iowa, Columbia and Bennington and is a professor emeritus of English at the University of Minnesota, where he taught for thirty-nine years and was a member of the Academy of Distinguished Teachers. He was the first Kilian McDonnell Writer-in-Residence at the Collegeville Institute at Saint John's University, and in 2014 received the Graven Award from Wartburg College.